3 4028 08047 3581
HARRIS COUNTY PUBLIC LIBRARY

J 591.5 Ben
Bennett, Artie
Poopendous! : the inside
scoop on every type and
use of poop
$16.99
ocn740631269
1st ed.   08/01/2012

WITHDRAWN

D1289929

To Dr. Seuss, my meuss.
—A.B.

For Kristin, Patrick, and Matthew—I love you.
—M.M.

TEXT COPYRIGHT © 2012 ARTIE BENNETT

ILLUSTRATIONS COPYRIGHT © 2012 MIKE MORAN

ALL RIGHTS RESERVED/CIP DATA IS AVAILABLE.

PUBLISHED IN THE UNITED STATES 2012 BY

🍎 BLUE APPLE BOOKS

515 VALLEY STREET, MAPLEWOOD, NJ 07040

WWW.BLUEAPPLEBOOKS.COM

FIRST EDITION 03/12   PRINTED IN DONGGUAN, CHINA

ISBN: 978-1-60905-190-7

2 4 6 8 10 9 7 5 3 1

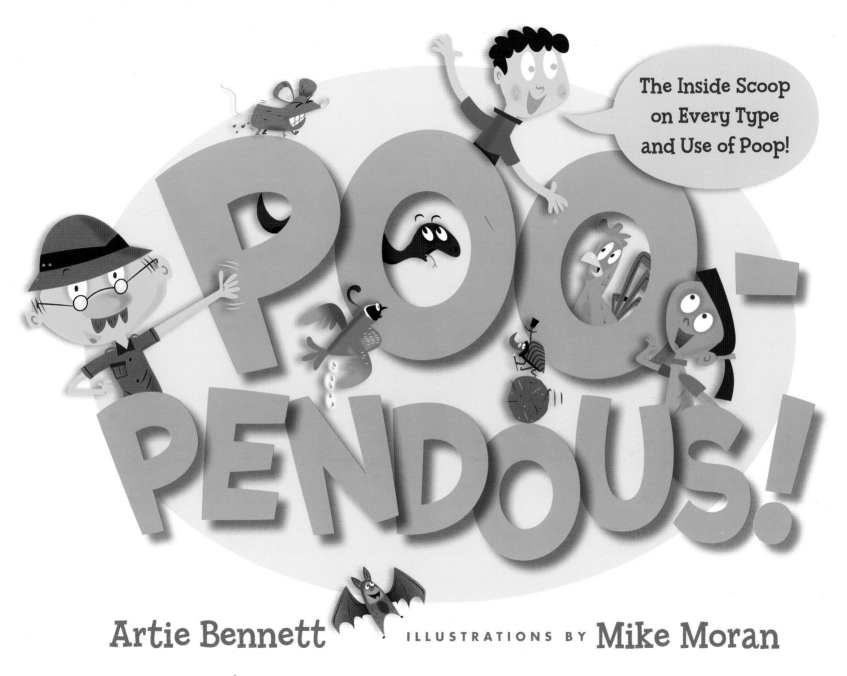

POO-PENDOUS!

The Inside Scoop on Every Type and Use of Poop!

Artie Bennett   ILLUSTRATIONS BY Mike Moran

BLUE APPLE

PROFESSOR P. POOPDECK

I'm Professor Pip Poopdeck. Welcome aboard!
We're exploring a substance that most have ignored.
An icky-poo subject folks don't care to visit.
Quite putrid and shocking and horrid . . . *or is it?*

Poop is yucky, poop is foul.
Step in poop and you will howl.

To read this book, you must be strong.
Just hold your nose and come along!

Everyone poops—yes, it's true—

From aardvarks

to the humped zebu.

And every creature in between.
It's simply part of life's routine.

Ca-ca, doo-doo, boom-boom, poo,
Are Baby's words for "number two."

Guano is an Incan word
For poop of bat or ocean bird.

Poop from critters is called dung,
And monkey dung is sometimes flung.

Monkeys fling when under stress.
It helps the monkey decompress.

So if a monkey aims at you,
Duck behind a friend,
or two!

Your dog may bark to drop a clue—

She needs to do her doggy-doo.

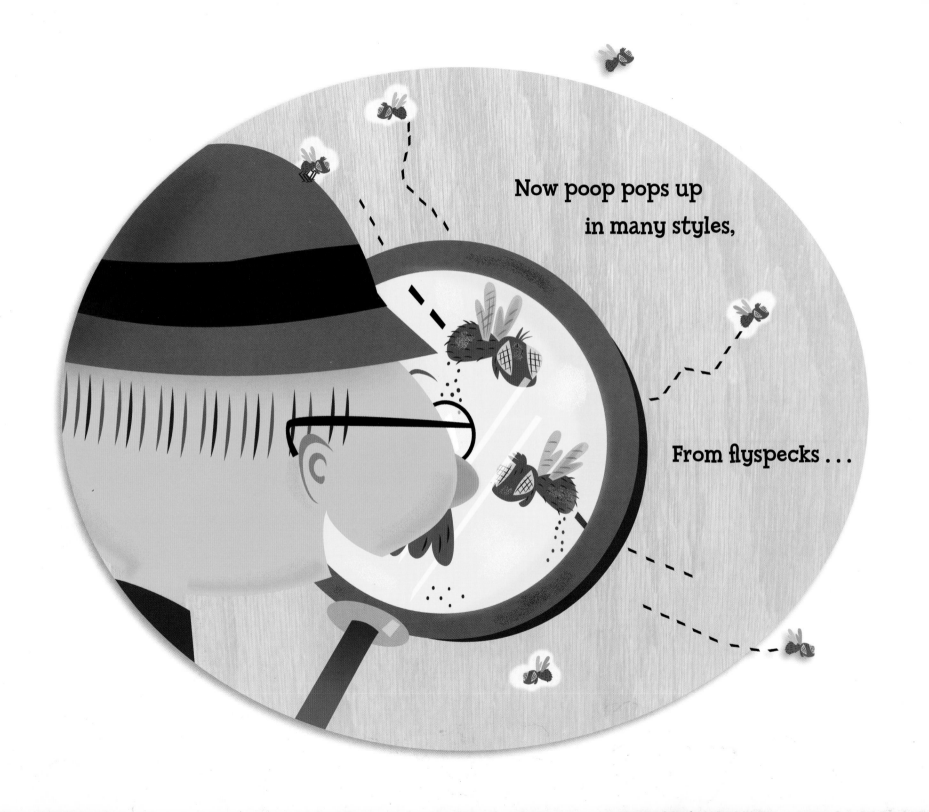

Now poop pops up
in many styles,

From flyspecks . . .

to great hippo piles.

Rabbit pellets, raccoon tubes,
Owl whitewash, and wombat cubes.

Camel poop is desert-dry.

Wet poop comes from birds on high.

A thought to fill us
all with dread:
"Oh, will that bird
poop on *my* head?"

DRUMROLL, PLEASE!

Let's introduce

The many ways dung is of use.

Termites found above the ground
Poop to make a mighty mound.

Dung beetles roll it into balls
To gobble up when hunger calls.

Guess how critters
    who feast on fruits
Help these plants
    to put down roots?

Seeds inside
   a critter's poop
Might go as far as
   Guadeloupe!

GUADELOUPE

Poop is helpful on the trail.
Is it bear . . . or is it quail?

Some use poop to mark their scent,
And let them know which way they went.

Or, poop deposits may convey:
This is MY turf—STAY AWAY!

Poop enriches soil that's poor.
Grow umpteen beans and greens galore!

If your crops are small and fewer,
"Hey, farmer, have you tried manure?"

Around the world, some folks you'll meet
Use dung for cooking and for heat.

The Mongol yurt,
    a native shack,
Is often sealed
    with dung of yak.

A Masai tribesman
    proudly struts
Before a row
    of cow-dung huts.

Moose poop makes great souvenirs.

Wear it dangling from your ears!

Some county fairs
have just the thing—
A thrill-filled, skill-filled,
cowpie fling!

Now you have the inside scoop
On every type and use of poop.

"Post Modern" CaCa

DA POOP

Not merely "Gross!"
"Revolting!" "Vile!"
Yes, poop can surely
be worthwhile!

Why should such
wondrous stuff offend us?

Poop is TRULY quite . . .

Harris County Public Library
Houston, Texas